Successful Negotiating in a week

PETER RONALD FLEMING

Hodder & Stoughton

A MEMBER OF THE HODDER HEADLINE GROUP

Dedicated To

Terry for her encouragement and patience.

Also available:
Successful Negotiating in a Week Cassette – ISBN 0 340 65468 0

Order queries; please contact Bookpoint Ltd, 39 Milton Park, Abingdon, Oxon OX14 4TD. Telephone: (44) 01235 400414, Fax: (44) 01235 400454. Lines are open from 9.00 - 6.00, Monday to Saturday, with a 24 hour mesage answering service. Email address: orders@bookpoint.co.uk

British Library Cataloguing in Publication Data
Fleming, Peter
 Successful Negotiating in a week. - (Business in a week)
 I. Title II. Series
 658.4

ISBN 0 340 70545 0

First published 1996
Second edition 1998
Impression number   10 9 8 7 6 5 4 3 2
Year   2003 2002 2001 2000 1999 1998

Cover photo from Telegraph Photo Library

Typeset by Multiplex Techniques
Printed in Great Britain for Hodder & Stoughton Educational, a division of Hodder Headline Plc, 338 Euston Road, London NW1 3BH by Cox & Wyman Ltd., Reading, Berkshire.

the Institute of Management

F O U N D A T I O N

The mission of the Institute of Management (IM) is to promote the art and science of management.

The Institute embraces all levels of management from student to chief executive and supports its own Foundation which provides a unique portfolio of services for all managers, enabling them to develop skills and achieve management excellence.

For information on the various levels and benefits of membership, please contact:

Department HS
Institute of Management
Cottingham Road
Corby
Northants NN17 1TT
Tel: 01536 204222
Fax: 01536 201651

This series is commissioned by the Institute of Management Foundation.

C O N T E N T S

Peter Fleming FIPM, FILDM, MC Inst M, is Managing Director of his own consultancy group – PFA – formed in 1982, and may be contacted at 01235 534124.

Amongst his portfolio of successful training programmes is Negotiating Skills which he has provided at Practical and Advanced levels for many executives and managers through the Institute of Management. With past experience in line management in the public sector, training management roles in distribution, and buying exposure in retailing, he has had considerable experience of negotiating at all levels and roles. He is Training Consultant to a major UK Trade Association and visiting Training Consultant at the Henley College of Management.

Peter is married with two children and lives in Oxfordshire.

Negotiating an unrepeatable deal is the dream of many people – whether it is a multi-million pound agreement which enhances the firm's 'bottom line' or the house purchase and sale which is the envy of our friends.

When good bargains are within everyone's sights, why is it that some people obtain much better results than others?

The fact is that there are no magic answers! However, we can identify key skills and approaches – used by experienced negotiators – which should help achieve better deals for all parties.

This book covers ten steps:

Ten steps to successful negotiation
- Create the right environment
- Research your objectives
- Decide who you are and who your opponent is
- Open the meeting
- Talk and listen
- Make proposals
- Summarise
- Close and confirm
- Evaluate strengths and weaknesses
- Continue your development

Remember that negotiating can be enjoyable. But there is no point in suggesting your opponents should negotiate – they may not have thought of it!

Prologue

Our attitude to negotiation is critical because it can make a substantial difference to how we see:

• the solution
• our 'opponents'
• the outcome we would like to achieve

"Super-deals" sometimes make the newspaper headlines but so too do disasters:

Unions flex muscles as bosses plan new pay round

"Multi-National" puts small supplier out of business

Super salesman sells 'dud' chemicals

Many people's reaction to such headlines is:

'If that is what it takes to be a negotiator, you can count me out!'

The fact is that, everyday, many millions of deals are struck which do *not* lead to strikes, breaches of contract, high court actions, divorces or suicides!

There is always a possibility, though, that something could go wrong – and it is wise to ask yourself about this *before* setting up a negotiating meeting.

> You will be more likely to be successful if you know how to create the right environment for negotiation to take place.

Creating the right environment

This is our first step in preparing for a negotiation.

It involves:

- Creating the right **atmosphere**
- Choosing the right **time** to negotiate
- Selecting the best **place**

We must remember that we may have to negotiate at short notice and, although we may have had little or no time for preparation, it is still important to play by the rules!

Creating the right atmosphere

Experienced negotiators recognise that there are four possible outcomes to a negotiation:

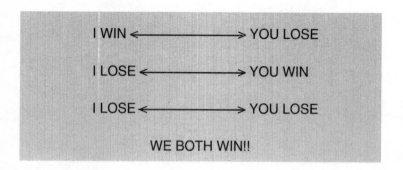

I WIN ←————→ YOU LOSE

I LOSE ←————→ YOU WIN

I LOSE ←————→ YOU LOSE

WE BOTH WIN!!

Most people would prefer not to be losers normally —
unless they have other motives — and the risk of 'losing',
divides negotiators into two categories:

- those who are **competitive** and want to win at
  everything
- those who are **collaborative** and want to achieve the
  best deal for both or all parties

If your role or aim is the continuing development of your
business, goodwill or relationships, the second style will
bring better, long-lasting relationships *and* results!

So, the right atmosphere will be affected by:

- How you feel about the situation
- How you feel about your opponent
- The relative power of the two parties
- Your ability to cope with stressful situations
- Your composure – especially with emotional pressure
- How much you trust each other
- Your degree of open-mindedness
- Your aspirations
  (Are you the sort of person who would wish to achieve better-than-average results?)
- How prepared you are to listen (as well as speak!)
- Your charisma.

Incidentally, our use of the word 'opponent' does not mean 'pistols at dawn'! It is simply a shorthand word to describe the person with whom we are negotiating!

Remember that, if you want to achieve a win/win deal, your opponent needs to **want** to arrive at a satisfactory agreement too.

You can influence this by the way you use the ten factors above.

Choosing the right time

The 'right time' to negotiate is probably when you have least need for a deal and your opponent's need is greater. However, collaborative negotiators minimise the 'fall-out' from such relationships. Otherwise, the opponent may feel 'beaten' and determined to beat you next time. Warfare of this kind can go on for years!

Skilled negotiators:

- choose their timing carefully
  (avoid the 'bull-in-a-china-shop' approach)
- patiently draw reluctant opponents to the negotiating table (it could take time)
- avoid spontaneous negotiation sessions
  (if at all possible!)
- prepare their case carefully
- weigh up what they think may be on their opponent's agenda
- know their own limitations and those of their opponents
  (for example – are you 'sharper' in the mornings or in the evenings?).

Selecting the best place

The right place to negotiate is any place where you feel most comfortable and, as important, most confident!

This comfort factor involves more than just feeling at home when your own 'home territory' could provide you with disadvantages as well as advantages.

For example, you would prefer not to:

- be distracted by minor queries while trying to concentrate on the negotiation
- be interrupted by telephone calls
- allow your opponents to see the state of your workplace
  (it could be chaotic or perhaps somewhat luxurious in their eyes! This might not impress them!)

These factors may help to heighten their confidence and lower yours.

On the other hand, witnessing these events on your opponents' ground may help you quite a lot.

'Neutral territory' is often suggested by negotiators as an appropriate way of avoiding any bias in the meeting.

However, you should beware of:

- neutral territory which subsequently turns out to be your opponents' home ground
- being 'landed' in a situation in which you are far from comfortable.

Social situations can put some negotiators at a disadvantage, for example being invited to a more up-market restaurant than you might ever have visited previously for a business negotiation.

Perhaps having to work in very cramped conditions, with very loud furnishings, might unsettle some people.

Summary

So, let's summarise our progress today:

- you should think carefully about how to build a partnership with your opponent
- look inside your heart and ask yourself: 'Am I really seeking a win/win outcome?'
- when will be the best time to negotiate?
- are we/is our opponent in a hurry?
- how can we use time to our mutual benefit?
- what advantages are there in going to the other party to negotiate or asking them to come to us?

These questions may seem obvious but the art of negotiating lies in applying them to your own situation.

Try to relate them to a current project or need.

For example, you may be thinking of changing your car.

Which of these points might be of greatest help to you today?

ATMOSPHERE	TIME	PLACE
....	....	....
....	....	....
....	....	....
....	....	....

Researching your objectives

Have you ever considered when the worst time for the week's food shopping might be?

Is it:

- when the store is busiest?
- when stock is running out?
- when you are in a hurry?

If concern about impulse purchasing is uppermost in your mind, the answer has to be:

- when you are hungry!

Of course, you might always prepare a list before starting the shopping expedition – some people do – but many others do not. If you stand and observe your fellow shoppers at the checkout you can quickly identify those who probably did not bring a shopping list!

There is nothing wrong with buying products we like, but was this a conscious decision or was the final bill a shock? The objective shopper starts out with a checklist and then consciously buys items not on the list.

Similarly, the skilled negotiator always prepares a checklist of objectives – a 'shopping list'– and uses it to compare actual results from meetings with those expected. Any move away from the original plan is then a conscious decision and a target for trading-off concessions from the opponent.

Skilled negotiators rarely negotiate without any kind of plan – and most produce detailed plans on anything but the back of an envelope or cigarette packet!

Preparing your own 'shopping list'

Preparing for a dinner party you are going to host may involve some or all of the following:

- deciding on a menu
- preparing a list of ingredients
- making a list of jobs to be done (and by whom)
- drawing up a seating plan
- sending out invitations

Similarly, a decision to move house should lead us to prepare an objective plan. For example, you may have decided to move to a larger house – 3-bedroomed, semi-detached with a garage – from your present 2-bedroomed

terraced house. You will probably start with a 'wish list' for the 'new' house which might read as follows:

- 2 double bedrooms, 1 single
- 2 reception rooms downstairs
- a downstairs cloakroom
- separate garage – close to the house
- gas-fired central heating

Of course, these items are not negotiable – they either exist or they do not – but their priority may vary and your view may be very different from that of your partner!

We rarely find exactly what we want and this listing will probably provide an important basis for negotiation at home before you even visit a prospective vendor. The result of these discussions will be a base line of standards or objectives, against which various offers will be screened. Probably you will not then want to visit properties which do not come up to those expectations (although this is by no means certain – did your present accommodation exactly match your 'minimum' standards?).

Preparing your negotiation brief

Once you have selected a property which you find attractive, you will need to produce a negotiating brief both for your purchase and your sale (if you have a property to sell). This will be two-dimensional and encompass:

- your objectives
- your best assessment of your opponent's objectives

Planning your objectives

Establishing your own objectives will be relatively easy. Taking price as an example, the buyer's objective will be to obtain good value for money bearing in mind the need not to exceed 'market value'. The buyer's parameters for price will be determined by:

At the 'top end':

- available funds – from the sale of a current property
- any bridging finance available (e.g. from your firm)
- a personal loan from your favourite Aunt
- how much you really want the property

At the 'lower end':

- the lowest price you feel the vendor might consider without insulting him/her and causing the withdrawal of the property
- the price which you feel correctly matches current market activity
- a price which enables the vendor to meet his/her plans

Assessing your opponent's objectives

Assessing your opponent's objectives means carrying out some research – at best; and guessing – at worst!

The process requires the ability of putting yourself in your opponent's position. For example, a vendor may have chosen to advertise a property at £80,000. It would be surprising (and unusual) if this did not include a 'fall-back position' which would allow for the agent's advice and the fact that some (if not all) potential buyers may make a lower offer.

So, the parameters for the sale may vary between:

(a) Price

Base Limit   Ideal Position

£ 72,000 ⟵——————————————⟶ £80,000

The 'base limit' here represents 10% discount on the asking price and could be lower if the vendor is desperate to sell, or if some fault is discovered in the building survey.

(b) Timing

Base Limit   Ideal Position

5/14th April ⟵——————————————⟶ 3/31st May

(This would allow for a holiday between 16th and 30th April)

Of course, there is a lot more at stake when we buy a house
– e.g. how well our own furniture will fit into it and what it
will 'feel' like when we are living there. Vendors are often
keen to sell items of furnishings such as carpets and curtains
and this can be very helpful if the move is a strictly
budgeted affair. Expensive mistakes can be made here too:

(c) Furnishing & Fittings

Bottom Line	Ideal Position
Vendor 'gives' contents away ⟵————⟶ with agreed house purchase	Buyer pays vendor's valuation of £7,500 for contents

As we shall see later, goodwill between buyer and seller
may have quite an effect in arriving at the most appropriate
point of 'balance' between the two extremes on the chart.
Any breakdown or loss of confidence between the parties
can lead to a Lose/Lose outcome.

Examples of Lose/Lose results could be:

- either party changing their mind and withdrawing from
  the transaction (leaving one party, or possibly both,
  considerable professional fees to pay – and nothing to
  show for them)
- carpets and curtains (etc) put into store rather than
  given away (leading to increased costs for the vendor)
- some items 'taken' by the vendor when the buyer
  expected them to be included in the price (leading to a
  rearguard action for restitution)

The effect of time

Time can have a crucial effect on the negotiation process as
we shall see later in the week. However, suffice it to say here
that a vendor who is being moved by his company (with a
tight deadline) may be prepared to consider a lower offer, if
he is convinced that the contract can be speeded up (e.g. by
a cash sale).

Equally, the vendor who can arrange to put his house
contents into store (and is prepared to – bearing in mind his
firm's preparedness to pay the bill) may be prepared to meet
the buyer's timetable – especially when sales activity is
depressed.

How do you find out about such levers?

At its simplest, you need to ask!

- Friends and family, etc.
- Professional advisers (e.g. solicitors, agents, etc.)
- People who have moved recently
- Your opponent/his family/friends/staff, etc.

My opponent? "Surely he or she will not tell you the truth," you may say. That may be so, but exaggerations or understatements can easily be checked and, if proved to be 'economical with the truth', may risk the breaching of all trust between the parties.

The broader the issue on which you are likely to negotiate, the more valuable it is to consult a wide range of people. In commercial negotiations the following consulting checklist may prove useful:

- Past users of the product/service
- Other experienced buyers/sellers
- Present referees
- Comparison agencies/publications
- Advisers
- Other people in your own organisation
  (the Japanese use this method to great effect –
  especially with new business contacts)
- Your opponent's own staff

So, your negotiation brief should include:

- an agenda of issues to discuss
- your objectives expressed in terms of parameters
- questions to ask to reveal information about the
  negotiation or your opponent's position

This is not paper for the sake of paper – a systematic approach will pay for itself over and over again!

Pre-meeting planning

The following checklist may help you avoid any loose ends:

OPENING

- How should I open the meeting?
- How interested are they in the meeting?
- What needs might exist?
  - Theirs
  - Ours
- What areas of common ground exist between us?

AUTHORITY

- Who am I meeting?
- What is the history/track record of the relationship?
- How much authority does my opponent have?

POWER AND INFLUENCE

- What is their 'power' over us and/or our competitors?
- What is our power in this situation?
- How can we exploit our strength for mutual benefit?

COMMITMENT

- How interested are they in the meeting?
- How badly do they need an agreement?
- Do we want/need agreement today?
- Will a negotiated agreement stick?

COMPETITION/EXCLUSIVITY

- How might market forces effect the negotiation?
- What leverage might be used?

INNOVATION AND PROMOTION

- What concessions are we likely to have to make to ensure the deal is successful?
- How innovative are the proposals under discussion?
- Who will contribute what to help?

Now that you have worked through Monday's text, why not try out your own plans for a car change, a house move or perhaps where you would prefer to spend your summer holidays.

Planning your objectives

Your Objectives   *'Opponent's'Position*

1 ....

2 ....

3 ....

4 ....

5 ....

Concessions You Can Give   *Concessions You Seek*

1 ....

2 ....

3 ....

4 ....

5 ....

Questions I Need To Ask

1 ....

2 ....

3 ....

4 ....

5 ....

People and places

Prologue

How able are you to persuade other people?

Some people are dismissive of sales people and would certainly not wish to sell as a career. Apart from the fact that the market economy depends upon a healthy marketing function for its success as an economic system, most of what we buy as consumers would not be available if it had not been for the efforts of salespeople in the distribution chain.

Negotiation is not about having blazing rows with your opponents – nor creating an icy atmosphere (although this might provide a possible tactic in certain circumstances!). The fact is that success in negotiation is really dependent on our ability to persuade other people and, in this respect, the sales person has a head start!

Think about your circle of friends and acquaintances. Do you know people with 'irresistible' personalities? People who always seem to be the centre of attention with no shortage of 'friends' wanting to support them, their ideas, be in their company, and do what they want? **Charisma** is a special quality but, sadly, it is rather rare and most of us have to manage without it. Furthermore, it is a gift and not necessarily enhanced by wearing designer clothes, the best aftershave or perfume!

Actually, persuading others is a skill which we use every day, with our families, our staff, our friends and colleagues, and (most important of all) our bosses!

Who am I?

Success in negotiation is affected by our ability to carry out the following skills and attributes. Rate yourself on this checklist:

FACTOR	LOW				HIGH	
I am the kind of person who:						
1 presents myself as a person who likes people	1	2	3	4	5	6
2 is positive (who wants to work with a negative person?)	1	2	3	4	5	6
3 is persistent ('No' can nearly always be turned into 'Maybe' and 'Maybe' into 'Yes')	1	2	3	4	5	6
4 is open-minded (there is always more than one way of achieving an objective)	1	2	3	4	5	6
5 develops a good sense of timing and tact	1	2	3	4	5	6
6 develops high aspirations for deals (skilled negotiators have high aspiration levels and tend to search for above-average agreements)	1	2	3	4	5	6
7 presents the case assertively (i.e. without waffle)	1	2	3	4	5	6
8 chooses the most persuasive words (use of vocabulary)	1	2	3	4	5	6
9 thinks clearly under stress	1	2	3	4	5	6
10 influences the emotional atmosphere of meetings	1	2	3	4	5	6
11 maintains self-control	1	2	3	4	5	6
12 takes decisions	1	2	3	4	5	6

On the above table, rate yourself against the factors by circling the figure which you feel represents your present skills.

We may not be good at **all** these things but, as this week progresses, awareness may encourage experimentation, and practice makes perfect! But, be careful not to experiment on live negotiations which could have a significant effect on your organisation's objectives – well, not yet, anyway!

Today's topic is about our personal effectiveness in relations with others and how to identify the strengths and weaknesses of your opponents.

Personal communications and negotiations

One facet of personal effectiveness, when it is applied in negotiations, is the use of an appropriate communications style. There are two specific styles which are used by us all in everyday communication:

- the extrovert style
- the inductive style

As may be readily deduced from the names, the first style is about our attempts to persuade the person to do something by giving lots of information – in effect, seeking to persuade by 'pushing' your opponent into a position.

The inductive style is concerned with trying to encourage your opponent to do something, by 'pulling' him or her towards that position. Clearly, this approach is more about manipulation and is more subtle than the extrovert style.

The extrovert style
Obvious characteristics of this style are shown below. This person:

- always has a say
- produces lots of ideas and suggestions
- may enjoy a discussion and argument
- quite likes to stir things up in a discussion
- may reveal inner thoughts regardless of the circumstances
- frequently gets his/her own way in conversations

The style also has a 'down side' which may dilute its effectiveness – especially in extreme cases! If opponents are to be *persuaded* rather than bludgeoned into submission, these factors need to be kept under control. The person may:

- take an aggressive approach to others
- call a 'spade a spade'
- give as good as he/she gets in an argument
- stick to a point of view having once expressed it
- criticise others
- look for all the snags and problems in new ideas

This style will be most successful, in the short-term, when negotiators are working in a powerful situation (i.e. power is on their side) and in a competitive climate. However, if the relationship is dependant on goodwill for its continuing success, there may be a greater likelihood of bruised feelings resulting from the negotiation. This, in turn, may lead to more aggressive tactics being used by the opponent next time (i.e. 'tit for tat') and the possibility of special 'favours' being offered to someone else if and when they become available!

Characters of the 'old school' who have developed a reputation of being strong negotiators – with a measure of charisma in their personal make-up – may attract a high level of respect from other people. This is particularly noticeable in competitive organisations and in sales oriented negotiations.

However, the style may not always transfer readily into non-aggressive environments and may lead to the isolation of the negotiator if the style is not appreciated by staff, senior managers, trade unionists or, indeed, customers!

The inductive style
As we have seen, this is the opposite communications style and, as such, tends to be rather less predictable than the extrovert style.

Its relative success is based on the principle that the more you are able to test out the attitudes and arguments of your opponents, the more likely you will be able to pinpoint weaknesses in their arguments. Indeed, the weaknesses may become clearer to them, thus enabling you to induce them to move towards your position!

Conversationally, the skills will involve the following:

- putting others at ease
- encouraging them to come up with lots of ideas
- being able to extend and develop those ideas
- encouraging a warm and friendly atmosphere
- giving credit and praise to others
- taking care to avoid upsetting others

Do you know people like this? How do you feel about being in discussions with them? Can you imagine your probable response if they were to ask for your help? Most of us would probably be pre-disposed to help them.

This effect is enhanced still further if you are also able to use clarifying behaviour in interactions with others, to ensure that there is a minimum of misunderstandings! This will involve:

- listening carefully to what others say
- checking that you have understood what they have been saying
- finding out what others are saying

and all this is possible if you

- ask lots of open questions!
  (These are the ones which start with What? When? Who? Why? Where? and How?)

These effects will be further enhanced if you are the sort of person who:

* admits to mistakes readily
* conciliates when things get heated
* admits to your weaknesses!

Finally, these skills should enable you to:

* obtain the information from others which you need in any negotiation situation

and all this will demonstrate the advantages of co-operating rather than competing with others!

Choosing a style

There is no perfect style which will work in every situation. Both styles have advantages – for example, a sales representative will need to be reasonably *extrovert* to survive the various 'knocks' from clients, especially when involved with canvassing!

Similarly, a negotiator involved in a much 'longer game', spread over, say, several months (e.g. the purchase of natural gas from the Norwegians), will need to adopt a softer, *inductive* role.

We should also bear in mind two other influences:

Making the relationship work
If your opponent is a natural extrovert who fills the time with lots of communication you may find yourself in competition for 'air time'. If this were to continue unabated,

it could lead to increasing frustration, over-talking each other and, eventually, conflict!

If two negotiators, whose natural styles lie in the extreme areas of the inductive style, were to meet to discuss a case there could be many questions asked by one party only to be met with more questions from the other!

In practice, styles tend to be a mix of both styles, with plenty of 'give and take'. In fact, the skilled negotiator will aim to develop expertise in both areas, so that he or she has complete flexibility and can move in and out of either approach depending on the needs of the opponent.

General cultural influences
Over the past decade in the UK, there has been a general move towards the inductive style in management and society in general. This may be attributable to a variety of influences:

- political neutralising of some of the aggressive influences in the industrial relations field
- increased awareness of the importance of meeting the needs of others
- effect of the human relations school of management theory
- increased effects and support of management training

Negotiators who are working in other cultures – perhaps in the Middle or Far East – need to adapt their style to suit the local customs and culture.

Who is my opponent?

We have seen that knowing something about your opponent before the meeting will be an advantage to any negotiator. So, having met the person before will enable us to be able to predict some of the possible levers and arguments which might be successful in the next round of discussions.

Aspects of communication style have already been discussed above and we will now consider possible 'pressure points' which could be applied to the debate.

All negotiations take place against an atmosphere of 'needs'; if needs did not exist then there would be little point in meeting to negotiate. To help you prepare for the meeting it would be helpful to consider the needs of your opponent in more depth. There may be a 'hidden agenda' which will help you select a negotiation strategy.

The famous Industrial Psychologist, Abraham Maslow, identified a **Hierarchy of Needs** to explain why people work in a modern industrialised environment:

The broad concept of the triangle is that we all have the need to survive, by satisfying the needs at the base of the triangle. Having satisfied these *physiological* needs our attention turns to the need for *security*, satisfied through the provision of adequate housing/accommodation. Both these factors may be satisfied through the earning of money but the higher motivators such as *social needs, status* and *self-fulfilment* are not normally satisfied in this way.

The model is shown as a triangle to illustrate the fact that not everybody reaches the higher needs – indeed some people become hooked on one particular need – or their ego just likes to be flattered under one of the headings.

For example your opponent may have a particularly 'soft spot' for good food and therefore may be a lot more malleable after a good meal (at your expense of course!). Others may be especially 'hooked' on status symbols and quickly identify your deal as one way in which they can be successful and earn a bigger company car or a status jump in the firm's hierarchy.

Equally manipulative is the industrial relations negotiator who holds a little in reserve to allow an opponent to feel victorious – just as the Union Branch is about to re-elect its representatives, or the Management is to consider the regrading of Personnel Professionals!

So where should we meet?

At first sight this is a common sense matter. Sales representatives might say they always expect to go to visit the buyer and the Management side of a Joint Industrial Council might always expect to hold meetings in the Boardroom.

Actually, the place of the meeting can make quite a difference to its 'comfort factor'. Some people seem to be able to fit into any environment and still behave confidently in business meetings. Others are intimidated by the very thought of having to negotiate on the opponent's ground!

So, playing 'home' or 'away' may have advantages to you and your opponent.

'Home' Advantages	**'Away' Advantages**
• you may feel more in control	• you have the chance of assessing your opponent's workplace
• you can control interruptions	
• you can orchestrate recesses	
• back-up support is available should you need it	• your opponent may make allowances as you are not on home ground
• you can choose your office/location/layout to suit you	• you can pressurise your opponent by suggesting senior staff get involved to break any deadlocks
• you may have the moral advantage in cases of late arrivals, etc.	

Another alternative is to choose 'neutral territory'. But, once again there may be some hidden advantages. For example the lobby of a hotel may appear to be neutral until you discover that your opponent is a regular visitor there and is personally known to the manager, the restaurant manager, the head porter, the barman and even the waitress. This can be most impressive – and is intended to be!

Will any of this make any difference to the meeting? It could do. After all, if you are dependent on your opponent for a crucial piece of information on which to base the negotiated agreement, would you mistrust someone who is so obviously credible in this sophisticated environment?

Plan Your Style
and
Negotiation Venue

What do you know about your opponents?

WHO WILL BE INVOLVED? ....

THEIR PREFERRED STYLE	YOUR PREFERRED STYLE
....	....
....	....

POSSIBLE VENUES

Home: ....   Away: ....
Neutral
Ground: ....

PEOPLE NEEDING A BRIEFING

....

....

....

....

Opening the meeting, and talking and listening

Now that we are half-way through the week it is time to meet our opponent!

Today we will consider how to open the meeting, and how to talk with impact, and develop our listening skills.

Prologue

We have now seen that good preparation is essential for effective negotiation meetings but it would be surprising if good presentation did not also play a major part in achieving good results!

Charismatic negotiators can be tempted to achieve their results solely through their force of personality and interpersonal skills. Most of us, however, need to be good at both!

Today introduces our opponent and the early stages of the meeting:

- Opening the meeting
- Talking and listening

As with our earlier days' work, we will find that a common sense approach to these two areas is sometimes overlooked by less experienced negotiators. Later parts of the meeting may well be affected by this so it is important to establish the meeting on the right footing, at the start.

Results from the opening, and the development of the early
stages of the meeting, will be affected by the following
factors. Before working through today's pages, you might
like to rate your current skills in each of these areas. Please
circle the rating which you feel applies:

Factor	Rarely Used				Always Used
• Establishing rapport – verbal and non-verbal	1	2	3	4	5
• Establishing common ground	1	2	3	4	5
• Exploring mutual objectives for the meeting	1	2	3	4	5
• Building a joint agenda	1	2	3	4	5
• Getting comfortable	1	2	3	4	5
• Clarity of speech	1	2	3	4	5
• Assertive behaviour	1	2	3	4	5
• Avoidance of bias and tunnel-vision	1	2	3	4	5
• Maintaining flexibility	1	2	3	4	5
• Listening for overtones and signals	1	2	3	4	5
• Questioning skills	1	2	3	4	5
• Controlling and reading body language	1	2	3	4	5

Your performance in each of these areas can be improved
and will affect your results!

Opening the meeting

Creating the right atmosphere for the meeting will be important if later parts of the meeting are to end in agreement. Tough issues can be sorted out without necessarily establishing an ice-cold atmosphere at the start; equally, if the players have not met before and the stakes are high, quite a time may be allocated to establishing an atmosphere of trust.

Two parties of two negotiators from businesses in the finance sector met recently for the first time to discuss transfer charges between their two organisations. Millions of pounds were at stake and, from the start, it was obvious that both sides were nervous about the possibility of making expensive mistakes!

To the surprise of both teams when they met in the hotel room, all the participants looked similar, were of similar ages, had dressed alike, and came from similar backgrounds. All this became increasingly evident in the first 45 minutes of the meeting which covered almost any topic except that which the meeting was about!

At this point, almost instinctively, the parties felt they had built up a feeling of trust, and they started on the agenda! Progress was then rapid and, to everyone's surprise, the meeting concluded in 1.5 hours with a Win/Win agreement and a celebratory lunch! The agreement endured for a year and provided a sound basis for subsequent renewals.

Establishing rapport

Meeting people for the first time – or indeed greeting someone we have met before – is normally accompanied by an appropriate choice of words and actions.

OH, HI!

However, how these things are carried out can be significant.

Passing the time of day and, as important, using your opponent's name, is an accepted custom in greeting – just as shaking hands provides an acceptable way of expressing warmth to the other person. We make some hidden judgements on the basis of these greetings:

- the firmness of the handshake – the 'crusher' or the 'wet fish'!
- the distance of the parties when they shake hands
- the formality or informality of the greeting – varying from 'Good morning' to 'Hi' or 'G'day'
- the warmth of the facial expression when meeting e.g. smiles can be open or, perhaps, cynical
- the extent of eye contact – open and level, or hooded and uncertain
- there is also the appearance of the parties – the manner of dress, etc.

The golden rule in the area of appearance – for the best results – is to try not to breach any areas of preference on the part of your opponent! This is not to say that there is no room for individuals in negotiation – but, breaching areas of known inhibition can be dangerous and expensive (as many employees will know from the experience of asking the boss for a rise!).

Common ground

It is always easier negotiating with someone you have met before because you will have some knowledge of that person's domestic circumstances, leisure interests, last holiday and/or drive or motivation. The early stages of a meeting provide an excellent opportunity to 'catch up' with what has been happening with your various lives – domestically and, probably more importantly (from the point of view of the negotiation) recent business activities – since you last met.

This episode should help either party to rebuild common ground between you which may be especially valuable if (or when) the going gets tough later in the meeting.

Obviously, a new contact needs careful nurturing – and the opportunity should be taken to find out a little about each other – without creating the impression of being either nosey or pushy!

The agenda

It is surprising how often negotiators meet together – with a mutual interest in meeting – but without having established a common agenda at the start. This is probably because each negotiator tends to think of his own agenda as of paramount importance and superior to the other person's interests.

If the meeting is to be collaborative, then it is important to provide the opportunity for *both* participants to air their own agenda. Apart from anything else it is quite a challenge to check your opponent's agenda against the items you *expected* to be raised when you prepared for the meeting!

This does not mean that every agenda item or objective *has* to be revealed at the start of the meeting, but failure to do so in a collaborative atmosphere will invite the question 'Why was this item concealed? Was it really a slip of the memory or has some advantage been sought by failing to reveal the topic?'.

Physical comfort

Physical conditions of the meeting will also influence how comfortable (and possibly how co-operative) either party may feel and this can be readily transferred to comfort with the deal itself. A variety of tactics may be adopted to win 'unfair' advantage over the opponent. Mostly these only work when they are not too obvious and, by virtue of their exposure, they tend to become decreasingly effective.

Examples are:

- your opponent's chair set at a lower level to yours
- your opponent having to look into the sun (or bright light)
- orchestrating interruptions when the going gets rough
- manipulating the temperature of the meeting room
- choosing a venue for the meeting which has distracting furnishings (e.g. walls decorated in, say, a vivid blue can affect some people and may account for an opponent's willingness to disagree with proposals)
- the rather prominent positioning of a clock which may give discussions a sense of time pressure

How should you deal with these tricks if and when they arise?

In short, the best method is to let your opponent see that you have noticed the tactic and seek his/her approval to remove the influence. This may be achieved by correcting or neutralising the influence and commenting on it to allow your opponent to understand that you have noticed the use of the tactic!

Talking and listening

The most obvious skills are sometimes those which cause most difficulty in meetings. The effect of the talking and listening process is affected by a variety of factors:

- self-discipline in being prepared to allow your opponent some 'air-time'
- the actual style we use in speaking (e.g. not too biased or self-opinionated)
- quality of listening – which is affected by factors such as interpretation and concentration
- our body language

Talking

From our earliest years talking is essential to our well-being but how we talk in a negotiation meeting can have quite an effect on how we are perceived by those we meet. For example the following request to the boss:

> 'I suppose it wouldn't be possible – I know this is probably not the best time to ask – to maybe find five minutes to get together to see if you could find your way clear to, perhaps, pay me an extra £5 per week?'

would probably be greeted by a simple . . .

. . . 'No!'

A great deal of work has been done recently on helping people develop assertiveness skills and this was a good example of non-assertive behaviour ... waffly, vague, apologetic and almost defeatist! Few skilled negotiators would contemplate using this approach!

Equally, making the following demand:

> 'If you don't pay the yard staff an extra £10 per week, you will be looking for a new team!'

could result in the response

> 'If that's your attitude then perhaps that is the best thing for us to do!'

Skilled negotiators are more likely to use the following approach:

1 Q: 'When will the Board be looking at this year's pay review?'

2 A: 'It is scheduled for consideration in March.'

1 Q: 'How much are you proposing to include in the budget?'

2 A/Q:'We will be under great pressure to find anything – given the present state of the market; how could the staff side make a contribution?'

1 A: 'If you are talking about productivity improvement, the staff need money on the table! However, if you have something to offer there may be scope for discussion.'

Assertive expression is based on our needs; and the use of *we* is better than *I*. In fact, self-opinionated negotiators who use an egotistical approach often find it difficult to persuade others to change their minds or adopt their proposals.

Similarly, emotional responses are best kept under control. The use of anger, for example, can make a short-term point in a meeting but, if it is over-used it can obstruct a negotiated settlement – with a 'lose/lose' result. The golden rule is to keep cool, avoid rhetoric and provocative language and maintain self-control. This can be difficult if the opponent is hyped-up and determined to cause maximum disruption as a deliberate tactic. In such cases, a good defence is to slow interaction down, make a conscious effort to avoid reaction and concentrate on non-controversial language!

HEY, WOLF! LET'S LOOK AT SOME ALTERNATIVE STRATEGIES!

Listening

To say that it is essential to listen to interaction in negotiation meetings is to state the obvious. However, this can be harder than it seems. For a start, the process in any conversation can be difficult for some people; and when we are seeking a negotiated bargain it is complicated by the additional demands on our brain in the meeting.

Put simply, negotiator 1 makes a proposal to negotiator 2 who listens carefully to the point. However, as the statement is unfolding, negotiator 2 seeks to comprehend the point made – checking it against prior knowledge and experience and listening for the overtones in the expression – whilst also beginning to form a suitable reply and appropriate method (e.g. 'Shall I ask a question, make a statement or what?'). It is hardly surprising that points are missed in such circumstances – and sometimes our response may be totally irrelevant! (How well do you listen to your partner at home?)

Why else can it go wrong? People have a habit of 'tuning out' – especially if they do not want to hear what is being said (try telling your teenage children to tidy their bedrooms, for example!). Others turn a deaf ear, making the right sounds while their brain is really in 'neutral' and there is no real commitment to change!

And, lastly, we take the power of vocabulary for granted – especially the importance of using comprehensible language. Jargon, for example, needs to be avoided and it is essential that any which is *not* understood by the opponent is immediately clarified. Here, again, is another valuable use of assertive questioning.

Recipes for improving your listening skills include the following:

- watching your opponent's lips while they are talking (and watching their eyes while you are talking – to gauge their reaction to what you are saying)
- try concentrating on the over-riding message in their contributions – rather than becoming bogged-down or distracted by individual words
- take notes to aid your concentration
- avoid trying to second-guess your opponent's statements or trying to finish off their statements (even in unison!)
- categorising contributions received from your opponent (e.g. is this contribution a question, summary, or proposal – and planning an appropriate response)

These approaches will help your concentration and enable
you to spot opportunities for discussion and for bargaining.
For example, an innocuous discussion during the earlier
part of a meeting with a client might reveal that ...

1 '...yes, things have been pretty busy – we have just
   changed our computer'

2 'What kind of pressures has this brought? Strings of
   noughts on pay-slips?'

1 'No, but our bought ledger system has come to a halt'

If you are proposing to supply this customer with a service
or goods, then be careful. You could decide on a contract
easily enough but you may have a job to encourage the
client to pay up ! So, this signal should be followed up when
it comes to agree terms of the contract at the end of the
meeting.

There are many other ways of communicating:

Non-verbal communication

Body language, and the skills of reading it, has recently become a very popular topic amongst the business community. 'If we could read the minds of our opponents and be able to work out exactly what they are thinking and planning, we could achieve much better deals!' Unfortunately, it is not as easy as that because analysing body language is an imprecise science!

However, there are some simple signals which are useful to observe in negotiation, although the novice should be careful *not* to apply the meanings in a literal sense in every situation.

Face touches

It is said that in conversation about, say, the price of a service or goods, if the speaker accompanies a price quotation with a typical statement such as 'This is my best offer' with a rub of the nose, a scratch of the chin, a wipe of the eye or a tug at the collar, it may be an untruth! The chances of this will increase if a chain of these actions occur together. However, it should always be remembered that the speaker may have a cold (causing a constant nose irritation), or be feeling uncomfortable in a hot environment (hence the tug at the collar!).

The moral here is that, whilst it is sensible to observe and try to read your opponent's body language, it is best not to allow your hands too near your face whilst negotiating!

Mirroring

Two people who are anxious to make a good impression on each other with the aim of a win/win deal, may mirror each other's body position and movements. The explanation for this is that each party is sending signals to convince its opponent that both sides are very similar in terms of attitudes, values and aims.

This approach can have a significant effect, although it may only be sub-conscious! So, if your meeting is rather cold and you wish to try to relax your opponent, mirroring his/her body positioning may have a helpful effect.

Eye gaze

We saw earlier that level eye contact is often taken as an indication of honesty and, therefore, an interpretation could be that the negotiator may be trusted. However, eye gaze cannot be constant in one direction, or it may be interpreted as staring! Negotiators need to vary their use of eye contact but an essential use is to look for reaction to ideas or trial proposals. Failure to do this may protract a meeting – simply because the signals of possible progress in persuading the opponent to accept your position may go unnoticed. What signals? The occasional frown or flicker of a smile; the raising of an eyebrow or even the sharp return of a glance. We take many of these points for granted, but, if observed, they may help us interpret progress in the negotiation.

Hand movements

Many people talk with their hands and, whilst this is quite natural, it is important that such movements should not become extravagant or distracting to your opponent. A pen or pencil can provide a useful means of underlining a point – especially if the meeting has become emotional – but aggressive movements should be eliminated. Anything which causes irritation in an opponent is to be avoided as this may otherwise lead to non-acceptance of your proposals.

In general, open-handed expressions may be taken to underpin the sincerity of the speaker, whereas pointing or closed fists may reveal aggressive undertones in your opponent.

Review

Now that you have worked through Wednesday's chapter, go back to the checklist on page 47 and look again at those items which you marked lower than 4 or 5. Place a cross against the scores you would aim for in future negotiation meetings.

Proposing

Prologue

Negotiation meetings are about mutual needs. For example:

- you need to buy a new car and the dealer needs to sell one

or

- you need to obtain the re-instatement of a suspended work colleague and the management needs to obtain staff support for overtime to meet a rush order

On Wednesday we found that meeting discussions provide the opportunity for us to present *our* side of the case - to promote and defend our interests – to sell our position and the advantages of accepting it to the other side.

We will also have tried to draw from our opponent a description of their position so that we can begin to debate it, undermine it and make it seem impossible or unreasonable. Whilst this is going on, our opponent may be trying the same tactic on us!

For example, a standard tactic when surveying a secondhand car is to fault the car by referring to the high mileage, worn tyres or rust-marked body. This softening-up process is designed to precede the making of a proposal (often a rather low one!) but this tactic may be easily rebuffed if the vendor is prepared to claim the 'large number' of other potential buyers who have been in touch about the car! Is the buyer really interested, or not?

Assertive questions such as 'How can you justify this position?' may draw your opponent to reveal his or her arguments and aims in the negotiation. With persistent questions, difficulties in arriving at a mutually agreed strategy on his or her side may be revealed, thus enabling you to take the high moral ground or express the stronger (more persuasive) argument! Dividing your opponent from his or her side is easier once you know that there may have been some difficulty on their part in arriving at an agreed negotiating strategy.

Of course, such debating points are reversible and you must be careful not to lay yourself open to the use of this approach by your opponent. So, any attempts by the vendor of the car to sell it to your partner – who is loudly proclaiming enthusiasm for the vehicle – may cause you some difficulty when it comes to obtaining the best price or terms.

In reality, it is unlikely that your opponent will make any major moves for nothing, so you will have needed to demonstrate your preparedness to move in some way – as a means of obtaining movement on your opponent's side. These signals should have been sent and received before beginning to form the proposals which will lead to the final bargain.

Today's session describes how to maintain this process through the making of appropriate proposals. We will consider:

- Timing
- Encouranging proposals
- The best formula
- Defending principles
- Meeting inhibitions

All your preparation will prove its value in this vitally important stage.

Timing

There is a right time for proposals in a negotiation meeting and experienced negotiators sense when the moment is right. This sense of timing is akin to the sales person's ability to choose the right moment to close the sale. How we find this out, other than by trial and error, is analysed below.

Exhausting every avenue of discussion will leave you with a need to achieve progress in the meeting, and making proposals is the next obvious step. However, this stance can feel over-cautious and pedestrian, and may lead your opponent to become exasperated through lack of progress. (This can, of course, be turned to an advantage if your opponent is very anxious to conclude the meeting - a process which might be quicker if he or she makes some quick and major concessions.)

When your meeting concerns an urgent issue and either or both negotiators have a strong sense of destiny, there will be an irresistible force moving the discussion towards agreement – especially if the parties have already expressed a strong desire to reach an agreement. In such a situation, proposals will flow naturally almost as a summary of each party's position.

The reverse of this natural progression rests in the truism described by Professor Parkinson (ref: Parkinson's Law) – that time taken for decisions is in inverse proportion to the costs incurred. Committees have been known to spend hours taking decisions about the replacement of canteen cups but only minutes on major decisions which few members understand! The same can be true of negotiation, when small issues combine with ready quantities of time, progress in the meeting can be very slow – with as much attention given to the social objectives as the deal itself!

Finally, beware of the use of time as a major tactic in the meeting. Logical movement through the early stages of the meeting may be positively unattractive to so-called skilled negotiators and this fact may lead to one of them suggesting a jump from base square to final square in one move. A simple, innocuous question might be asked:

> 'We are both busy people and I am sure we could close this deal very quickly – if you agree, of course?'
> 'Yes, that seems a good idea.'
> 'So, what is your bottom line?'

Revealing this position may make it difficult for the opponent to trade movement once the base position has been revealed. There will then be little alternative to agreeing to the initiator's proposals – without breaking off negotiations altogether!

Encouraging proposals

If you feel that the time is right for proposals to be made but are not sure whether this feeling is mutual, you can always ask! Hand-holding skills are valuable in negotiation, i.e. encouraging the opponent to feel that you are trustworthy, and are not trying to lay a trap. Apart from giving the other side the opportunity to drive the meeting, encouraging them to make leading proposals in an open atmosphere will help progress to be made.

Such a step needs to be accompanied with appropriate non-verbal signals – warm smiles, gentle nods and a high level of attention (eye contact and slightly laid-back body position but facing the opponent).

The best formula

Phrasing for proposals is quite crucial. The best formula is to present your proposals using a conditional approach. For example -

> '*If* you will give us payment terms of 30 days,
> *then* we will meet your price request.'

Now, this proposal may seem rather bald – especially without examples of the earlier conversation! When a bridge is needed between the discussion part of the meeting and concluding the bargain, either party may introduce *trial proposals*. These will suggest tentative ways forward without necessarily burning our boats and risking earlier agreement by suggesting something which is not acceptable to the opponent.

A typical example would be:

> 'I'll tell you what we might be able to arrange, *if perhaps* you could find a way of speeding up payment – say, in 30 days - *then we might* be able to find a way of reducing the price.'

If this approach brings a constructive response, then it is likely to be followed swiftly by a formalised proposal along the lines of the first example above.

Defending principles and meeting inhibitions

It is at this stage that you may find your bottom line under attack or in threat of being compromised. For example, HM Government made it clear after the Falklands War that sovereignty was not even on the agenda for peace negotiations with Argentina and this would be a pre-condition for any future discussions.

There could be a risk that, whilst such a condition might be agreed, your opponent may reintroduce that element in the meeting itself, with the expectation that the constructive atmosphere might persuade negotiators to allow discussion of the issue. This clearly should not be accepted and the team would have to make it clear that approaches to put the subject on the agenda would jeopardise agreements on other issues.

At the same time, you must remember that your opponent is not an entirely free agent. He or she is representing another organisation or party, with interests which may be different from your own. These interests will overlap – or there will be no point in attending the meeting – but it is obviously in his or her interests to persuade you to move from your ideal position.

For example, a client may complain about one of your service engineers whose behaviour on his premises had been the source of complaint from several of his staff. His initial approach may be to demand the withdrawal of that person ('Never send him here again!') and this may be readily countered with an apology and a convincing promise to hold a full and thorough internal inquiry.

However, if we were to think through our opponent's position we would see that his organisation has in it several people who would also like to see the back of the engineer! Failure on his part to sort out the issue could lead to a significant loss of face and credibility for your opponent. Such inhibitions can lead to apparent obstinacy and may make a win/win agreement more difficult to achieve if the client's inhibitions are not addressed.

Summarising, closing & confirming

Prologue

There is little point in investing time in negotiation meetings if we cannot close them with satisfactory agreements. However, there are many people in the commercial world who make presentations with a view to sell a product or service, or buyers who invest time in meeting with sales representatives and those meetings do not result in a contract!

The question is, do those involved ever discover why their closing rate is not higher? And can they do anything about it? In staff relations meetings there is less priority given to immediate results – often meetings are broken by recesses and adjournments – and consultations between staff representatives and their members and personnel staff and their managers. But the same disciplines apply here – if time is invested in meetings, then agreement must be the ultimate objective.

So, what are the skills we need to develop in closing off a negotiation meeting satisfactorily? The following checklist may provide useful insights:

- Summarising progress
- Resurrecting earlier issues for agreement
- Using concessions to improve the agreement
- Choosing appropriate persuasion strategies
- Linking issues in the agreement
- Listening for concessions
- Using appropriate closing techniques.

Mistakes at the 'last fence' can be very expensive and frustrating!
Make sure you are able to clear the last few hurdles cleanly so that you are satisfied with your performance!

Summarising

One little word!

It is not possible to do too much summarising in a meeting; the fact is that many people become confused during negotiations and, even though one party has a clear belief on what has been agreed, it often happens that the opponent has a very different view of that same agreement! Both people were at the same meeting and yet there is still confusion and little unanimity – and this is very dangerous when the agreement is actually implemented!

Examples of things going wrong, after the negotiations have stopped, are legion. Buyers select colours of merchandise and plainly state the colours they do not want – and yet, somehow, those colours still arrive in deliveries! Similarly, sales representatives inform buyers about discount terms and yet they still claim they have not been told about these points after the invoice arrives.

Summaries help to clarify proposals and the terms of agreement. You cannot do too much of it! Remember the one little word which provides the signal of a summary – *so*, ... and try to use it:

* whenever the progress of the meeting is stuck
* when you are not sure what has been said or agreed
* when you feel that the time is ready to begin to close the meeting

Accuracy in summaries

When summaries are used in a meeting they can have an extraordinary effect! Firstly, a summary often seems to fix the points stated and agreed – even though both sides know that the discussion is not yet finished. This can be very helpful when seeking to make speedy progress but it is important for the summary to be accurate. If you include in your summary something which has *not* been agreed – even if you feel that you are taking artistic licence – there is a risk that the relationship between the two parties will be broken and trust breached.

Similarly, it is very important to listen to summaries given by your opponent. There is always a risk that something you believe has been agreed is left out or changed in the opponent's summary. If this should occur it is important that the party who spots the error speaks out straight away.

Otherwise the change may be accepted into the agreement by default, and could cause a major disruption towards the end of the meeting with a possible emotional effect on both parties. This might not affect the ultimate agreement but it might leave either or both parties with a bad taste in the mouth, with a knock-on effect on future meetings.

Resurrection
By virtue of the fact that a strategic summary will be seen as a means of bringing the meeting towards a close, it provides a last opportunity to raise any items on which no progress was made earlier.

Remember on Tuesday we talked about persistence being an important quality for negotiators? The fact is that people who refuse to move earlier in a meeting may be a little more flexible when the end of the meeting is in sight. Also, the presentation of your case and the subtle temptation of concessions may encourage your opponent to be more flexible on issues which were sticking points before.

Linking
Linking one item with another is a further method of obtaining movement on difficult issues. Most negotiators see their agenda as consisting of a variety of separate issues or objectives – indeed many commercial deals involve the sale and purchase of several products or items, each of which needs to have been negotiated. It would be quite normal for the negotiators to achieve different deals on each item on the list but it is also likely that either side may resist giving way on one particular item. A way out of this is to link one issue with another.

For example, a buyer may have agreed to pay a wholesaler £11.00 for a box of 5 reams of photocopying paper with an order of 100 boxes. He is pleased with this agreement as the price agreed is 50p a box less than he had expected to have to pay. Another item on his shopping list is some specialised bond paper for use in preparing and presenting reports. The wholesaler has offered a price of £18.00 a box which the buyer is unprepared to agree – his counter offer is £16.00. On the basis of negotiating the same quantity of paper, the buyer offers to increase the price on the copy paper by 25p per box if the vendor will agree to a price of £16.00 for the bond.

Remember that everything is negotiable and you just need to persuade the other side to accept this to make progress with issues on which your opponent has inhibitions!

Using concessions

Concessions may provide a way of obtaining additional movement towards the end of the meeting. Skilled negotiators know to keep additional concessions up their sleeves to use in closing the meeting. These will be most effective where the concessions are cheap for you to give but very valuable to your opponent.

For example, if you have just sold your car – and therefore have cleared the cheque – you may be able to persuade your garage to extend the warranty on a new car for the all-in price which you agreed earlier, but now with the additional concession of a cash transaction.

Closing

Sales people are frequently trained to close the sale and a variety of methods exist to help achieve just that! However, if negotiators have done their job well the meeting will close itself. The best resolution of the meeting is when both parties have achieved what they set out to achieve (ie within the parameters of their objectives) and all that is left to do is to formalise the agreement.

This may not always happen so it is sometimes necessary for the meeting to be nudged towards closure. The following checklist shows some common ways of achieving this:

- Calling a recess
- Imposing a deadline
- Threats to pull out or call time
- Asking for agreement
- The summary close.

Calling a recess
The forming of a decision about, and therefore a commitment to, the agreement which has been discussed often requires a little time and space. Reluctance for your opponent to agree to the deal may be overcome by planting the seeds of satisfaction in his or her mind and then allowing time for thought (with a view to allowing the seed to mature and flourish). If you have covered the ground well and summarised the areas of agreement, a short recess at this stage should bring a positive decision.

Imposing a deadline

If there is any doubt about the result of the recess it might be prudent to lay down some rules about the time for which the current offer will be valid. Clearly this approach may be viewed as pressurising your opponent – but is quite justifiable when the time period is fair.

A typical example could be a quotation for a construction task which is dependent on the supply of the materials – and the quotation assumes no price rises for the materials – therefore the quoted price can only be valid for, say, one month.

Threats to pull out

If one party believes that the other party *needs* the agreement, then a bluff to pull out of the meeting may work. However, such orchestrated tactics can easily rebound on the bluffer if the timing or style of the threat is tactless. You might easily find that you are allowed to go and not called back!

SORRY- I HAVE TO SEE SOMEONE MORE IMPORTANT

On the other hand, it has been known for creative answers to be found to situations where the time has run out on the negotiating.

For example, when international negotiators spent 18 months trying to negotiate a Strategic Arms Limitation Treaty, and the self-imposed deadline was reached, the parties agreed to stop the clock for 36 hours – just sufficient time for the final agreement to be transacted. When they finished, the agreement was back-dated to fit the original deadline!

Asking for agreement

A simple way of closing the deal is to ask for your opponent's agreement! At first sight this is such an obvious approach that it may be unclear why everyone doesn't use it all the time. 'Asking for the order' is a classic technique taught on most sales training courses. However, sales people do not often use the approach, simply because of the risks of being turned down.

Actually, a turn-down may not be the disaster it may seem. It may be possible to rescue the deal even at a late stage simply by asking 'Why?'. The answer may clarify your opponent's objections giving you one last chance to bring the negotiation to a satisfactory conclusion.

The summary close
Finally, the closing point for the meeting should be summarised. The skills for this have been described earlier today.

A cautionary note!
Don't forget that your opponent enjoys a free will to agree or not to agree! Even though you may have worked hard and concluded a good deal, your opponent is still acting for his or her reasons not yours. This may be worth bearing in mind if you are feeling euphoric when you start to evaluate the deal!

Confirming

Even when your meeting seems to have closed with a full-hearted agreement, there are still risks that the implementation of the agreement is faulty. The success of the negotiation lies in this process and it is probably hard – with the euphoria of a successful outcome – to turn our minds to what can go wrong.

However, things *do* go wrong, often for no sinister reason. The parties' recollection of what was agreed may be inadequate but if the performance of the agreement does not meet either sides' expectations it would be quite understandable if underlying motives were questioned.

Solutions to avoiding these problems include:

- Taking and exchanging notes
- Getting the agreement in writing
- Checking that minutes and opponent's notes agree with your notes
- Taking care with the small print

Taking and exchanging notes

It isn't easy to contribute to a negotiation meeting – talking, listening *and* making notes, but working notes of the meeting will be an essential foundation for any subsequent agreement or contract. In the commercial world, it is quite usual for a representative's memorandum of sale and a buyer's order to be drafted during the meeting, and exchanged at the end. This provides the first check that both sides have a common understanding of what has been agreed and, with experience and trust built up over time, one side may be prepared to accept the other's notes.

In staff relations meetings it is common for both parties to nominate their own secretary to take minutes of the meeting and the notes are then used to form the ultimate record of the meeting.

Get it in writing!
Even when notes have been exchanged at the end of the
meeting it is still important for a *formal record* of the
agreement to be exchanged. Most negotiations commit two
organisations as well as the various players and formal
records will need to be exchanged.

Confirmations may take the form of:

- Purchase requisitions
- Sales order notes
- Letters of confirmation
- Revised proposals (bringing letters of acceptance)
- Formal contracts
- Joint communiqués or treaties
- Procedural agreements and bargains

A cautionary check is to ask yourself:

> 'Am I covered in law if anything should go wrong?
>   Who could I sue?'

This is not to say that you would wish to – *most* disputes
between contractors are resolved by negotiation. But skilled
negotiators will not put themselves into a position where
they have no recourse if the opponent should renege on the
agreement.

Check confirmations agree with your notes
How often have you attended meetings and failed to
recognise the minutes when they have been released some
time later? Unfortunately, those who have the responsibility
to prepare the notes are sometimes tempted to misuse that
power to rewrite them to suit their preferred position –

subsequent to the meeting. Even if this is not intended, subtle changes may take place to meet the political inhibitions of the boss, the organisation or even some of the people present. Where changes have been noted, and where these affect the letter or spirit of the agreement, a loud complaint should be made, officially. Any apathy here may be taken as acceptance of the new situation!

Take care with the small print

One major company in the North of England employs a whole department of lawyers whose main task is to check buying agreements and ensure that their own terms and conditions are supreme over those of their suppliers. The consequence of this is that any small supplier is unlikely to be able to achieve any variation to those terms and may be faced with the stark choice of contracting on the buyer's terms or not at all.

We would all prefer that breakdowns do not lead to recourse to the law – this could be very expensive in time and money – but the larger the contract the better it would be to ensure that the worst consequences of failure do not leave you totally exposed to losses as a result. For this reason, penalty clauses are often found in construction contracts, restraint of trade in personal contracts and even clauses allowing actions for damages against trade union bodies where the continuity of supply of a service is affected by a trade dispute.

Evaluating performance and continuing to grow

Whilst there is little point in crying over spilt milk, there is no doubt that we can learn from past mistakes. Indeed, it is likely that all negotiators have made mistakes at some time or other – what is unforgivable is to make the same mistakes over again!

Consider the following checklist which may help you pin-point your own strengths and weaknesses:

Preparation
1 Do I spend enough time preparing to negotiate?
2 Have I discussed the case with other people in my organisation?
3 Have I researched my opponent's case?
4 Is there any additional information I may be able to collect from my opponent's organisation?
5 Which outcome do I really want:

   Win/Win, Win/Lose or Lose/Lose?

6 Have I prepared a negotiation plan/brief?
7 What is on my objectives/shopping list?
   What are the parameters for each objective?
8 Have I prioritised my objectives?
9 What concessions can I give?
10 Where will we meet?
11 Have I analysed relative power positions of our two organisations?
12 When will be the best time to meet?

Know yourself

13 In what circumstances am I:
- most comfortable?
- least comfortable?

14 How easy do I find it to:
- take decisions?
- persuade others?
- be positive and persistent?
- choose the most persuasive words?
- think clearly under stress?
- control myself?

15 What motivates me?
   What 'Achilles Heels' might exist in me?

16 Am I a disciplined listener?

17 Am I tempted by a win/lose opportunity if I will be the winner?

Opening the meeting

18 How good am I at putting others at ease?

19 How good are my presentation skills?

20 Can I control and read body language?

21 How able am I at probing others for information?

22 Can I respond to others' probing without giving away anything of value?

23 How well am I able to develop a collaborative atmosphere in the meeting?

24 Have we established a common agenda and identified common ground?

The meeting

25 How well can I balance talking and listening?

26 How can I make the meeting layout work for me?

27 How good are my concentration and listening skills?

28 When might a recess be useful?

29 How can I make good use of interruptions?

30 Who is in control in the meeting?

31 Have I identified the best time to make proposals?

32 How good am I at introducing trial proposals?

33 How can I formulate counter-proposals to overtake opponent's proposals?

34 Am I using 'If...then' and 'So' successfully?

35 When my opponent blocks my proposals, am I able to unblock them again?

36 How able am I in using closing skills:

- hand-holding?
- summarising?
- using late concessions?
- linking?

Don't forget that the real test of your negotiation meeting lies in the results.

Skilled negotiators have:

- a track record of significant success
- a low incidence of failure in the implementation of their agreements
- high ratings for effectiveness by both sides

Continuing to grow

Negotiation is a practical skill. It is subject to the same characteristics as other skills – it gets rusty if it is not used – and improves and is sharper when used frequently. So, there are a number of steps which the negotiator can take to increase these skills:

- Take every opportunity to negotiate
- Talk about negotiation with experienced people both inside and outside your organisation
- Read about negotiation – look at
  - newspaper articles for recent cases
  - trade magazines for technical sources
  - books and articles
- Review your deals carefully and thoroughly
- Attend a training course which enables you to obtain some feedback about your style and skills (preferably through the use of cctv). We look forward to meeting you soon on one of our workshops!

The truth is rarely pleasant and the review process will be pointless if you indulge in a form of self-kidology! Check your objectives and those known about your opponent – and make sure you do not make the same mistakes twice! Happy and successful negotiating!

Reading list

Finally, the following books will enable you to extend your knowledge of this subject further:

General

Skills of Negotiating,   Bill Scott
Managing Negotiations,   Kennedy, Benson, MacMillan

Advanced Skills

Negotiating: the Better Deal, Peter Fleming

Commercial/Sales

Negotiate to Close,   Gary Karrass
Bargaining for Results,   John Winkler
Getting to Yes,   Roger Ury
Retail Selling,   Peter Fleming
Managing Retail Sales,   Peter Fleming

Industrial Relations

Effective Negotiation,   Alan Fowler

Personal Skills

Assertiveness at Work,   Ken & Kate Back